Overheard In St Andrews

Zella Publishing

Copyright © 2012 Zella Publishing

All rights reserved.

ISBN-10: 1477640460
ISBN-13: 978-1477640463

DEDICATION

To all the students, locals, and tourists of St Andrews who made this text possible.

CONTENTS

1 Pour Out Some Dom   9

2 Sensual St Andrews   27

3 LASH   38

4 Academic Prowess   49

5 Town Livin'   69

6 Tourists, Locals, Kids   96

Introduction

    An illustration of the more subliminal attitudes in St Andrews not seen in golf books or student guides is given by these hilarious conversations between students, locals, and tourists. These raw excerpts shatter the often lofty air given to the town by its grandiose history and royal past, providing a glimpse of the real life in "the bubble."
    For the passing student who wishes to see or remember the St Andrews "uni life," for the local seeking to grasp what adds the color to their town, to the tourist who wants to see what's beyond the 18th hole, may this book of conversations as reported by students provide that fresh understanding.

Pour Out Some Dom

Two guys, in Westport:
1: "Mate, what the hell are you wearing?"
2: "I'm Scandinavian. I do whatever the f*** I want."

> **Guy in the queue waiting for buses after May Ball:**
> **"It's like the f***ing Titanic lifeboats."**

"I can't decide which of my parents credit cards to use."

Guy on South Street:

"It's so annoying when you get people who don't normally fly first class, and they're just playing around with their seats and things like that..."

Third year guy trying to convince drunk girl to pass out in his bed rather than his flatmate's:

"I mean, go ahead and sleep in his bed if you want to, but my sheets have a higher thread count. Just saying."

After the May Dip:

Naked guy: Where's my tweed? Has anyone seen my tweed?"

"You're my working-class friend."

> **A guy is grinding behind a girl, and as she turns around with a disgusted look on her face, he says:**
> **"It's okay, I'm in the Kate Kennedy Club!"**

"My family were badly hit by the recession, we had to get a Land Rover Discovery instead of another Range Rover."

"When people intimidate me, I just think 'I'm a member of the aristocracy!' and then I feel better."

On Hope Street:

"I'm seriously having a major panic here. The two pieces of my bow tie fell apart and no one can put them back together. Do you know anyone who could fix it, otherwise our night is ruined!"

**Girl: "Can I just say that I did not apply here to find a rich husband?"
Guy: "And I didn't come here to marry a poor girl."**

On The Scores:

"Of course I have first world problems, I live in the first world!"

Girl one: Look at the highland cows
Girl two: Oh, Daddy bought me a herd of highland cows for my eighteenth...

Guy1: "What you doing for spring break?"
Guy2: "Ugh I'm going to my Chalet in Switzerland, but it's so much effort to get there."

> **Guy: In library, after girl has just killed a bug on the table using a 10pound note:**
> **Friend:** "Ugh it's got spider bits on it now...what are you going to do about that?"
> **Girl (shrugs):** "Probably just throw it out. I mean, it's only a tenner."

"What would you do if you hypothetically woke up with £10 million in your bank account?"
Girl: "I'd wonder what happened to the rest of my money..."

Between McIntosh Hall and Hope Street:

"I spend therefore I am."

English Lecturer: "Who's someone you would call 'millionaire'? ... Some of you may call him daddy."

St. Andrews Lizard Lounge:
Doorman: £3 please.
Girl: Thanks.
Doorman: £3 please.
Girl 2: Thanks.
Doorman: £3 please.
Girl 3: Thanks.
Doorman: £9 please.
Girl 4: What?? Why? They all just paid £3 each!
Doorman: Aye but you have a patent Mulberry. £9 please.

"I've got Moët all over my guitar."

Outraged Swedish girl: "They don't sell Dior at Boots!"

Senior lecturer gives posh male student lift to Leuchars station- Posh student gets in lecturer's compact Nissan and immediately asks:

"Is this your wife's car?"

Prospective student on Bell Street to her mum:
"Oh, there is a Jack Wills and a Joules! Looks like I might be able to survive here after all..."

Girl from Hong Kong: "I used to have an Indonesian helper, but Filipinos are better."
Girl 2: "Okay...we have a house cleaner that comes once or twice a week. So I guess that's similar."
Girl 1: "Wait? You're helper doesn't live with you???"
Girl 2: "What about their families?"
Girl 1: "Well see, that was actually a problem. We had to keep changing helpers since they kept wanting to get married."

Girl 1 : "Don't worry, it's just an exam. Nothing in the grand scheme of life."
Girl 2 :"It'll be fine. Three semesters more to sort my s**t out- Get thin, engaged and a first. Simples."

Two girls walking across the zebra crossing at Church Square:
Girl 1: "URGHHHH. This is so annoying! My longchamp bag strap keeps sliding off the shoulder of my barbour jacket!"
Girl 2: (nodding) "life is hard."

Group of drunk guys on Hope street, chanting:
"We are the 1%! We are the 1%!"

"This is going to sound like such a middle class problem but...how do you get a bus?"

Girl in Sallies last night: "I'm at university to find a husband. And getting a degree is a back-up plan, in case he dies or something."

American girl in the queue for the Tesco cashpoint:

"It's getting so cold! I'm going to have to ask mummy and daddy for about 100 pounds more for taxis."
(Meanwhile, her friend, on leaving the cashpoint, forgets the 30 pounds she's just withdrawn)

Two drunk girls on South Street during Halloween, one in a pig costume, the other in a cat or mouse costume:
Cat girl: "So that means I only have a couple of weekends, Christmas holidays and Easter holidays to find my future husband!"
Pig girl: "Definitely, you'd better get shagging."

> **Guy having lunch in Rendezvous chatting on his iphone:**
> **"So he says he doesn't like wine OR cheese. Basically, I'm like, so why did you even COME to St Andrews??"**

Welsh girl in Regs:

"I think I'm just gonna work for a bit, and then get married and just be a housewife... I just can't be bothered."

"I can't...I have to go and book a polo lesson."

> **While buying an assortment of cheeses in a store:**
> **Girl 1:** "Well, it seems that we are going to have ourselves a cheese evening.."
> **Girl 2:** "A cheevening, so to speak."

American second year (female), outside the library:

"Selfless? Is that even a word? It doesn't sound like a word..."

Two American girls in New Hall:
1. You know, the British airports are really ineffective. I mean, who has 5 terminals for one airport?
2. "Yeah I know what you mean. All the stores were in one terminal and my flight left from another. I nearly missed my plane cause I couldn't decide between 2 pairs of shoes."

"And I said to him like you can still climb the social ladder and be friends with people who aren't American."

A guy earnestly asking a girl in the short loan section:
"Can I marry you? ... I'll give you money."

Male yah on South Street: "She's amazing but I'm just not prepared to date anyone under 5'7."

Person 1: "So I was standing on the beach floor."
Person 2: "...You mean the sand?"
Person 1: "Oh yes...to you commoners."

Yah girl, facebook stalking in the library:

"She looks quite weird, doesn't she? I mean... (lowers voice) she looks like she's on BENEFITS or something."

12:34am, The Library, Blonde girl in heels:

"Now it's time for me to walk and be seen."

Man in fetching tweed jacket and red trousers on South Street:

"I left some Empire outside my flat, for you know, the proles."

Outside the library, 11pm (in American accent, loudly):

"I like him much better now I have seen his car."

Girl in Tesco: "My dad gave me £200, cos he said God forbid that I drink cheap sparkling wine"

Loud drunken guy in tail coat outside Nisa after the may dip:

"This god damn labour government wont sell me champagne at six in the morning!!"

Watching Titanic – Two guys walk by:
Guy 1: "What part are you at?"
Guy 2: "Oh this is the bit where they leave the good party to go party with poor people!"

Person 1: "What are those things called, the things that are all black?"
Person 2: "Destiny's Child?"

Girl on market street (sobbing):

"But I want to be a magician SO MUCH!"

Two girls behind me in Tesco:
Girl 1: "My mum's really upset I'm not coming home for Easter."
Girl 2: "Yeah, mine's upset too but I'm not coming home until I find a husband."

Sensual St Andrews

"I mean it just gets so boring here...sleeping with people becomes the only form of real excitement."

"It's hard. She's in Melville and I'm on North Street but we make it work."

> **Girl on market street, loudly:**
> **"So then I woke up and was like oops... wrong twin!"**

Boy: "The problem is, people actually want to sleep with boys in the KK."
Confused girl: "What?"
Boy: "Well, you wouldn't get all this fuss about the Lumsden Club, because they all look like potatoes."

Girl in Westport Court: "Sex is very good exercise."
Boyfriend: "Yeah it is."
Girl: "Not if it's only for a few minutes…"

A girl on Hope Street:

"He called me the next day and was like, 'So I just wanted you to know that the condom broke. Do with that what you will.' DO WITH THAT WHAT YOU WILL? Who says that?"

During revision week in the library:

"She only wants to have sex with me at the moment to have something else to do. I feel like a procrastitute."

Girl to her boyfriend:
"Aw, please? If you let me do the dishes, I'll have sex with you."

In line at Costa Coffee:
Guy 1: "Did you see her last night?"
Guy 2: "Yeah."
Guy 1: "Did she cook you breakfast?"
Guy 2: "No..."
Guy 1: "Did you cook her breakfast?"
Guy 2: "No, we didn't have any breakfast."
Guy 1: "Were you still with her around breakfast time?"
Guy 2: "I guess so."
Guy 1: "You realize this question isn't really about breakfast, right?"
Guy 2: "Well, you keep using the word 'breakfast.'"

Girl 1: Oh!
Girl 2: What?
Girl 1: Ah...
Girl 2: Hmm?
Girl 1: I just thought that guy was really fit...then I remembered that I've had sex with him.
Girl 2: Brush your shoulders off.

Guy in regs: "I like you in clothes. It's like a challenge."

Guy in new hall... "Are you Catholic or prostitute?"

"If you've kissed someone and slept with them, but don't really know them, should you give them a Christmas Present?"

In a stairwell of Andrew Melville:

"Look, I just want to know if he actually tea-bagged me, because I'm just not okay with that."

British girl: "So you said never to date Indian guys, right?"
Indian girl: "Right."
British girl: "What about Pakistani guys?"
Indian girl: "Hmm, no."
British girl: "Okay, what about Arab guys?"
Indian girl: *pauses* "Depends how much money they have."

Market street between a guy and a girl:
"I feel like going to church.."
"...Reaaaally?"
"Yeah. I want to pray for happiness.... And by happiness I mean a really hot guy..."

Lecturer in second-year English: "I'll make her a shape poem. Ladies love shapes."

American girl in mermaid ball queue:
"And I am like what-up gingerbread latte, how you doing?"

Girl in desperation over guy issues:

"I don't know if he's not interested, or just nerdy and doesn't know what to do with boobs."

Outside Tesco:
Girl: "What's up...."
Guy: "If I tell you wats up will you sit on it?"

Girl on phone on South Street:

"Yes, of course I remember what happened, I still have the stains on my dress."

Guy 1: "Dude I f***ing hate Halloween."
Guy 2: "Why?"
Guy 1: "I'm still pulling cobwebs out of my mouth from that girl I hooked up with."

Toastie bar– a girl and guy (1) have been ostensibly making out while waiting for their orders. Girl leaves to go talk to a friend:
Onlooker to Guy 1: "That guy is telling her not to do it. You should go break them up."
Guy 1: "It's ok, I've got her toastie numbers and her purse."
Onlooker: "You are a man of power."

"No not the Lizard, the last time I went there I went home with a Scottish Guy!!" Said in utter shame and horror.

Two people in St. Mary's Quad:
Girl: "You should really come to the Bop this weekend."
Boy: "I don't think I can. I have an academic family meal."
Girl: "Well, just bring them all along. We're kind of related anyway."
Boy: "... How?"
Girl: "Well.... we did sleep together once."

Girl on phone heading to union: "Have you got [name]'s number? I think I'm drunk enough that I can f*** him again."

Awkward guy and girl on South Street, Freshers, drunk, post-Union closing:
Guy: So like, I've got no where to go now.
Girl: Well, you could come back to mine, for... you know...
Guy: *silence*

Geography lab: "No I won't sleep with ALL the guys. One has a girlfriend!"

On South Street, post-May Ball:
Girl to sleazy guy: "I'm really sorry, I would invite you back to mine, but I really want to watch the new Doctor Who on iPlayer..."

> **"When it comes to describing personality you can be 'bubbly', or 'happy' – He's just 'rapey.'"**

Boy in line waiting to give blood turns to girl behind him:
"Did I spoon you on Friday?"
Girl "Yes."
Boy "Oh good"

"I'm not a slut, I'm just really... vulnerable."

Two madras girls on queens terrace:
"Are you gonna shag him then?"
"Probably- but only if he stops smoking... and listening to Miley Cyrus."

LASH

Suited man after being told not to smoke indoors at the Christmas ball:

"I always smoke after sex."

Guy walks into Melville at 8am:
Girl: "Walk of shame?"
Guy: "No, walk of glory!"

Yorkshireman on Argyle St; "If I ever meet Prince William, whether he's king or not, I'm going to ask him the most important question of all; Empire, Marmaris or KFB?"

Drunk male ordering/slurring at the Union bar last night:
Guy: "I'd like 2 chillies and 4 chicken nuggets please. *pause* That doesn't make sense does it?"
Barstaff: "No, not at all"
Guy: "'In that case I'll just have 2 chillies please."

Girl 1: "Tonight I just want to have a quiet night with a bottle of wine."
Girl 2: "Between us?"
Girl 1: "...each."

"If you want a girl to put out, you suggest going to the Lizard. She'll then know that sleeping with you at least means she doesn't have to go there."

Outside of Dervish:
Man in white pimp suit:

BITCHES WE BE GOING TO THE RULE!
stomps pimp cane on ground

In Greyfriars Gardens a guy puts his arm around a drunk girl:

"You know I'm running for President."

In Starbucks: Barista yells "Grande espresso for He-Who-Must-Not-Be-Named!" and a posh-looking post-graduate student shouts "YES!" grabs his drink and walks out.

Guy: "The doctor said I have an STD, but I don't believe him."

Guy: "So, I had to take a very business-like approach to ending my dry spell – I lowered my standards. Significantly."

Two rather posh guys in the queue in Boots
Guy 1: "So you just told her to get the f*** out of your flat this morning?"
Guy 2: "Yeah! dude, if she doesn't even know how to make eggs benedict..."

Man outside union, holding a bucket of water, to a group of people smoking: "Ladies and Gentleman, would you kindly stop standing in this lovely pile of chunder."

In the Union at 2am- Drunk guy staggers up to semi-drunk girl and chucks his arm round her:
"Hello. It's late... you'll do!"
SLAP.

Conversation between a student and lecturer over a pint:
Student: "So since the masturbation notice was a fake….is it allowed in the library?"
Lecturer: "Well as long as you're not excessively loud, and don't get the books too damp, I don't see why not."

"Having a prostitute is so much cheaper than a girlfriend."

In the Tesco booze isle (on Raisin):
"I thought she liked me, dude you TOLD me she wanted to f*** me."
"But that was a WHOLE BEER ago, we just gotta move on from these things in our past."

Three guys walking down greyfriars:
"I just saw the police break up a human pyramid outside Tescos."

Two guys, drunk on Market Street:
Guy 1: "What's that clock say?"
Guy 2 *after much effort*: "23:54??"
Guy 1: "Calm down dude. I'm too drunk to deal with numbers higher than like 10 right now..."

In the Union:
"Sooo I am studying medicine... and I was just wondering if I could get a sample of your saliva?"

> **Girl walking towards DRA, car pulls up beside her:**
> **Passenger: "I want directions... into your pants"**
> **Girl: "If you don't have sat nav you're not worth it!" *walks on***

American girl in Tesco- Looks unsure at her bottle of champagne:

"I wanna remember tonight..."

Gap Yah Guy on phone outside library:
"So you coming tonight? Yeah? It's going to be an absolute snogathon!"

Cold Caller: "Congratulations! Your postcode has been selected..."
Flatmate: "OK..oh...wait a minute...the condom's fallen off the wall"
Cold Caller: "Umm..."
Flatmate: "Sorry, just talking to my flatmate. What were you saying?"
Cold Caller: "Erm...it doesn't matter sir"
Hangs Up

Hope street guy: "You shut your whore mouth! This is a democracy!"

A group of American Freshers get stopped by the police outside Rymans for drinking in the street. One fresher decides to argue with the police by shouting:

"How can drinking outside be anti-social, if anything I'm being sociable!"

Two guys in front of the union:

"Yah mate, my flat is an ABSOLUTE disaster...like, I don't know how we'll manage to clean it up, because, yah, there's like champagne ALL OVER the ceiling"

White American fresher walking down corridor in Uni Hall to equally white neighbors: "Catch y'all n@£$as later!"

Outside the Vic on Wednesday night:

"What's the number for 999 in Scotland?"

At the union:
Guy1: "So how do you know her?"
Guy2: "I slept with her."
Guy1: "Me too!"
Guy2: "High five!"

On South Street:

"I guess you could call me the muffin man. Cos I brought you a muffin... and I'm a man."

Guy 1: "Whoever does the most outrageous thing on the night out gets the spare bed. The rest of you can sleep on the floor."
Guy 2: "Is sleeping with your mum outrageous enough?"
Guy 1: "Nah not really. She could probably do with a shag to be honest."

Academic Prowess

"GOD HAVE MERCY"

– Carved in exam table.

> **May Dip:**
> **Guy 1 (freaking out): "SH*T I have a Latin test tomorrow! I have a Latin test tomorrow!"**
> **Guy 2: "Carpe Diem, mate!"**
> **Guy 1: "What does that mean?!"**

Read on exam desk: "If Carlsberg did exams, it would definitely not be like this."

Philosophy student at house party: "I party therefore I am."

Overheard at the back of the exam hall, one invigilator to another:
Guy 1:"That guy over there needs to go to the bathroom when the other one gets back."
Guy 2 "Which one?"
Guy 1: "The effeminate one" -complete with hand motion.

Guy outside Lower College Hall yesterday waiting for an exam:

"To be honest, I still have no idea what the module is about."

English: "My subject is nothing but thinly veiled references to sex."
Biology: "Really? Mine is pretty explicit about it."

"I used to think that ibid was a classical author. Like Ovid, but Ibid."

> **"Sometimes I sit in lectures and open the BNP website on my laptop to see what the reaction of people behind me will be."**

"I put the 's' in 'literacy.'"

"Euripides, Cicero, cunnilingus, it's all the same. "I don't study classics."

Economics lecture:

A girl raises her hand and asks a question...in Chinese...

Lad 1: "So do you want to come to the party tonight?"
Lad 2: "I'd love to. I'd LOVE to. However I've actually got VIP space on the top floor of Club Library."

"Who's Kony? I thought he was someone running in the student elections..."

Tutor leaving for a board meeting:

"Now I gotta go drink champagne and snort some coke off a stripper. See ya guys next week."

At the Union
Guy 1: "You know computer sci take students to some god forsaken castle every year or something..."
Guy 2: "Computer Sci?!"
Guy 1: "Yeah, Physics and Maths do it too"
Guy 2: "What for? So they can get out into the sunlight?"

In medical school toilets, 2 actors talking:
"Oh hey, haven't seen you in a while! What's wrong with you this time?"
"Hiya! I've got terminal cancer, what about you?"
"Oh really? I'm obese and refusing to change my lifestyle."

"You couldn't possibly know her...she does computer science."

In New Hall:

"Does the Circle of Life become the Sphere of Life in 3D?"

> **Senior International Relations Lecturer:** "I think we should give all the Nuclear weapons in the world to Wales."
> **Inquisitive Student:** "The country or the animal?"
> **SIRL:** "The country!!! We want Japan to continue to exist do we not?"

Brilliant IR pickup line at Aikmans:

"Are you a constructivist? 'Cause I'd like to build a whole new world with you ♥."

Guy: "I am so glad exams are over..."
Girl: "Me too, I can finally iron my bed-sheets."

Hushed on the 2nd floor of the library: "Well this LIBRARY is a violation of my fundamental human rights!"

Posh girls walking to the library:
1. "Oh my god, I'm going to have to see my advisor and he'll be like, we're so chucking you out of this course, for, just, like, not doing any work."
2. "Oh my god no, he'll totally just be like 'I'm so sorry for that, like, nasty email I sent you, we love you."

End of exam at 11:30 AM:
Proctor: "Go have a glass of wine"

Library:
Guy: "Do you know we've got to answer five essay questions tomorrow and not two?! I just got the email..."
Guy: "...JOKE"
Girl: "I HATE YOU" *hyperventilates and cries*

Completely serious fresher: "but surely the cold war had to have been before global warming?"

Ancient history lecturer on elephants in battle:
"Elephants are hard to steer. The only thing harder to steer is an aircraft carrier... or a Death Star."

Girl in New Hall heading to put something in the bin:

"Ah, there's a bin inside a bin! Binception!"

In the physics café:.
Guy 1: My rule is always eat a f***tonne at Christmas.
Guy 2: Is that an S.I unit?

On a paper left in a book checked out from Short Loan:
"You know you like me
Go on lick me.
Smell me
Fondle with my pages
mmmm!"

"If you looked at a picture of the sun for a while, would you still go blind?"

Fairly posh English girl on computer in library, on phone:

"No Daddy, no no, I don't need help with the essay, I'm fine, honestly!" Then proceeds to spend at least twenty minutes listening and furiously typing, before discreetly murmuring:

"After 9/11, did we go into Iraq or Afghanistan?"

Guy working in the library, his friend joins him and asks: "What's that diagram you're drawing there?"
Guy 2: "Oh, I'm just trying to figure out how a foursome would work"

A male economics lecturer:
"In a duopoly, two firms can differentiate their products in multiple ways. Airlines, for instance, can have different timetables, different airports, different stewardesses..."

"A book!? I haven't read a book in 2 years!"

Girl in library: "I don't get why WWI was only called World War at the time"
Guy: "doubt they predicted a 2nd..."

Philosophy Lecturer: "So, suppose two people simultaneously shot Justin Bieber in the heart..."

3rd year Maths Student: "Well 16/20 isn't bad, it's nearly 85%"
Other 3rd year Maths Student: "Yeah, I know, It's 80%"

Zest, a group of people at a table
Guy: "They asked me to name my favorite architect, so I said "Ted Mosby."

In the cheese section of Tesco:

"From a strictly cardiovascular point of view, 40 minutes on an erg is a much better than 40 minutes in bed."

Guy on the phone outside the library:
"Yeah so I think what you should do is copy and paste a whole section from Wikipedia into your essay, and then go back on Wikipedia and edit it so it says something completely different. ... isn't that a good idea? ......[pause while friend replies]........ yeah that's what I did!!!"

Girl: "so he moved to Prague in the end."
Guy: "but it's so expensive there! At least, I heard it was expensive in Austria."
Girl: "Prague isn't in Austria?"
Guy: "Well, Poland then, whatever."

Outside the library:
Girl: "...so basically I'm already prepared for my tutorial!"
Long pause
Boy: "...I completed Batman Arkham Asylum last night."

> **American girl walking through market street:**
>
> **"I hate those moments when you realize you're actually stupid."**

In West Port:

"Suicide bombing doesn't really strike me as a career"

1st year history student in the library:

"So for the whole first two weeks when they were talking about that Martin Luther guy in lectures, I was totally confused and thought they meant Martin Luther King... but he has the same birthday as me so I'm doing my essay on him."

A girl this morning outside the Shell garage-
"Gosh, all these people actually go to their 9am's ?!"

"I usually think of my personal relationships in terms of neoclassical economic theory."

Girl in the library:

"This isn't working anymore, you can't write a philosophy essay without alcohol. I'm going to Tesco, be right back"

An Asian overseas student: "cummon, the ocean in St Andrews isn't that cold, it's just the Atlantic!"
Friend: "The Atlantic??"
Asian overseas student: "Well, the Pacific then, whatever!"

Girl 1; "I feel stupid next to you IR people, all I learn about is mushroom sex."
Girl 2: "At least you're going to have a job after four years."
Girl 1: "Yes. Watching mushrooms have sex."

Girl in DRA:
"So... what's up with this Gandalf in Libya?"

"Some people die harvesting our bananas........that would make them... BLOOD BANANAS!!!"

Girl on Butts Wynd:

"Oxford rejected my postgrad application by email! By email! I mean, that's just low. That's like the academic version of being dumped by text."

Outside Uni Hall:

Guy: "So what was the Italian test like?"
Girl: "Surprise buttsex."

1st year IR lecturer:
"I've always found it tragically depressing that boys always try and dress like their fathers in St. Andrews"

Town Livin'

**Guy 1: "I am in a long distance relationship with my girlfriend.
Guy 2: "Where does she live?"
Guy 1: "DRA."**

> **In Regs, two American girls:**
> **"Someone kept stealing my conditioner so I swapped it with hair removal cream."**

Guy who sounded a bit like Napoleon Dynamite a while ago in Tesco:
"God, I wish they'd stop moving the vegetables around. It's really messing with my zen."

Subway employee:
"I hate subway. I'm dead inside."

Old Scottish Starbucks cashier taking names for free latte's says to Asian girl: "You better not make this hard."

English girl on Greyfriars to friend:

"Sorry darling, I've got to dash, my quails' eggs are on the boil!"

In Toastie Bar:

"This is like daycare for drunk people"

"I hated Kony before it was cool."

Girl "It's ok, I sprayed it with Dettol and killed all the bacteria"
Me "Dettol only kills 99%"
Girl "It's ok, I sprayed it twice so I killed 198%"

Well-dressed gentleman wearing tweed gently running down street shouting 'I shall tear you to pieces' -Typical St Andrews fight.

Short Canadian girl in St Regs in the common room:
"Did Jeremy Kyle invent the lie detector?"

> **Queen's Terrace**
> **Guy 1: I'm not a hipster, I just happened to like hipster things BEFORE they were hipster.**
> **Guy 2: So... you're a hipster?**
> **Guy 1: I AM NOT A HIPSTER!**

Girl in New Hall talking about her washing:

"If anyone has touched my stuff, I will touch them....in ways that will make them uncomfortable..."

Girl 1: "The girl's bathroom is so small and crowded."
Girl 2: "I know trying to get around each other is like tetris."

In Tesco:

"What the f* is the f***ing unexpected item in my bagging area? I'm never going to Tesco again."**

Guy - "Apparently high class prostitutes can earn 150k a year, no tax."
Girl - "Do they have a grad scheme?"

Guy in Maths lab:
"I'm finding a new place to live because my flatmate stole one of the collectable swords from my cabinet and put it in his cabinet and is telling everyone it is his own."

In Subway: "If you come in here and you don't sound like a farmer, we generally assume you're a student."

Two American guys in Beanscene:
1: "My girlfriend's making me toad-in-the-hole tonight."
2: "You're eating FROGS?"
1: (miserably) "Yeah, i guess it's a British thing."

Melville dining hall:
Guy 1: I am so annoyed! my cleaner always comes on a Tuesday, so I didn't have a wank today. You know what- the bloody woman never even came!

"I hate wanting to sneeze and not being able to. Its what I imagine death would feel like at the end of an unfulfilled life."

Norwegian in the library:

"I hate seeing all these hot guys, when I look disgusting. I should have done science- they all look this bad. I mean, Purdie- it's hardly a fashion show."

Girl in my corridor worried about housing next year:

"If we have to live on the streets will someone share a box with me?"

> "Sometimes I put on a one-sy and eat cornflakes out of an egg cup with a teaspoon to make me feel like a giant..."

A girl in Sallies last night..."She's so stale, I want to make her into croutons!"

> **Library top floor, young woman muttering under her breath, about the twentieth person to walk up to the same desk near mine, look behind it only to see a pile of books and papers that have been unattended for about an hour:**
> **"Death's too good for you, whoever you are..."**

In a flat on south street: 'you paid £96 for your teapot!! What is it made out of panda?!??'

BOY 1: ... This girl showed up at Christmas dinner, and she was a vegan.
BOY 2: Alright, vegetarians are not to be trusted, but vegans should be put down.

Overheard in McIntosh, "Meg...Meg! I would no doubt kill everyone in this room if it would make Santa real."

> **Two guys outside the union last night**
> **Guy 1:** "Hey! i know you!"
> **Guy 2:** "Umm do you?"
> **Guy 1:** "Yeah! you're famous!!"
> **Guy 2:** "I'm not famous... I just have an afro."

Guy on a stairwell in McIntosh: "I got 99 doughnuts cos a bitch ate one."

A French guy talking to a girl:
Girl: "You know, we could talk in French as well."
Guy: "Ah... are you from France?"
Girl: "No, I'm actually from Belgium."
Guy: "Ah... I'm so sorry..."

At a birthday party:

"You can tell what year people are in. First years go for the free drink, third years go for the free food."

1: "ooh we should do something Scottish on St Andrews Day"
2: "Drink?"
1: "Does margarita count although its mexican?"
2: "F*** it, it's alcohol– therefore Scottish!"

"What? Eggnog is a real thing? I thought it only existed in stories, like butterbeer."

> **Guy in medical school:**
>
> "I've lost everything in St Andrews except my virginity."

Friend outside the union: "Screw alcohol, I want cookie dough!" *runs across road*

Girl on south street: "I just watched this really inspirational episode of one tree hill and now I just REALLY want to try harder. I'm gonna sign up for everything."

In the principles garden:
Guy: "Yeah, the Kindle battery lasts for like 40 days.."
Girl: "Wasn't that Jesus?"

Very nervous looking girl walks into John Burnet which is a scene of chaos from the party of the night before with beer cans everywhere.
"Is this the School of Physics!?"

Two guys discussing two Chinese girls. One says to the other:

"Am I just really racist or are they actually twins?"

Girl being interviewed outside the quad by Bubble TV:
"I have one word to describe raisin. Parents. Are. Mean."

A girl in my kitchen: "Are all cups waterproof?"

"Imagine you open your eyes and the first thing you see is a turtle... a gigantic turtle..."

> **Drunk Freshers in the Tailend on Raisin Sunday:**
> **Girl (whilst crying): "Are we really, actually in Scotland right now?"**
> **Boy (attempting to console her):**
> **"Yes...yeah, we...are."**

"People who kill themselves by jumping in front of trains are so f***ing selfish. Find a cliff or something."

An undisclosed Raisin party attendee after downing a particularly foul mixture;
"There's a party in my mouth & all the guests are Hitler."

A girl on south street, after inhaling a considerable amount of helium out of a balloon proceeds to sing:

"They see me rollin', they hatin…"

Two lots of tourists asking the other police-on-patrol:

"What on earth is going on?!"
"Raisin."

"The night before raisin is like the opposite of Christmas!" - guy anticipating his morning wake-up

German guy asked Greek girl if she could get her water from Tesco after studying together. Girl comes back and gives him the bottle. German says: "Thank you! How much was the bottle?" Greek: "C'mon don't worry! You're German! You guys paid for it anyways!"

In a New Hall Corridor, talking about how we need to recharge our RFID room keys every few days:

"Does the magnet-y stuff run out?"

"Raisin last year was, like, my descent into depravity."

2 guys on Market Street:
Guy 1: "What do you call a singing computer?"
Guy 2: "I dunno?"
Guy 3: "A Dell."

Guy in the union talking about the shag, tag bop – "I don't like this, the room is full of ugly, desperate people."

On the corner of Argyle St:

"I need him to die so I can go to his funeral and look hot."

In Macintosh:
"Who is it that's working on their laptop in a stall in the men's bathroom? Are they still there?"

"With the students out of town no-one is buying the humus in Tesco!"

Guy in the DRA bistro:

"I really can't work it out... Why do squirrels still exist?"

Half of a phone call overheard in the boys locker room at the gym:

"Dude, problem. I don't think we can waterboard [Jim]..."

"Because its illegal!..."

"Just because its in your garden doesn't make it not illegal..."

"I don't THINK he can die..."

"We should probably get him to sign something first..."

"I suppose if it really comes down to it I can be a witness..."

Girl on South Street:

"You've actually been to DRA? And you WALKED there?!"

Girl: "Why did you choose the Royal Bank of Scotland over the other banks? Did it have the best deal?"
Guy: "Urm...not really, I just figured that because it was the 'Royal' Bank of Scotland, it was bound to better."

Girl in the DRA Laundry:
"I don't really wash my clothes very often, I just tend to spray them with air-freshener."

"I don't understand how Asians can smile and watch where they're going at the same time."

In Melville four guys start sprinting towards the kitchen.
Guy 1: "Are we running?"
Guy 2: "YES! THEY HAVE NUTELLA!"

Girl 1: "Yeah I fall in love with a different girl in the library every day."

Girl 2: "I know what you mean, they are so pretty and when you sit across from them all day you sort of get attached."

Girl 1: "Yeah and then they leave and your heart breaks…"

A fresher to her friend just by east sands:

"So… if West sands is looking out onto the North Sea, what sea is this?"

In the Union:
Girl 1: "Are you okay?"
Girl 2: "No I didnt get much sleep to be honest."
Girl 1: "Why?"
Girl 2: "I had a dream i was in Poundland... and something had a sticker on it saying £1.65.. more of a nightmare to be honest."
Girl 1: "I know how you feel."

In Tesco, 2 boys talking in the self-service queue:
Boy 1: "Hey, so do you think Gadaffi looks like Carlos Santana?"
Boy 2: "Who?"
Boy 1: "Carlos Santana, you know, the guy out of Led Zeppelin?"

1st year talking about one of the cleaners in New Hall:

"She probably uses Cif as a lubricant."

2 Guys in Northpoint:
Guy 1: "Gaddafi's dead."
Guy 2 : (with a look of serious concern on his face) "WHAT? You mean the guy from Ndubz?!?!?"

Girl with her friend in Tesco:
Girl 1: "Why are you taking 6 cucumbers??? We've only making salad for the two of us!"
Girl 2: "Weren't you listening when I told you I've given up on guys...?!?"
Girl 1: (awkward silence)

In Tesco:

"It's a pot noodle and a wank kind of night."

Girl leaving the cinema, slightly missing the point of Lion King 3D:
"I wouldn't have gone if I'd known it was going to be exactly the same..."

On the way back into Melville after a brisk 9pm fire alarm: "Next time they drag us out for no reason, I'm gonna set MYSELF on fire in protest."

At a house party:

"I just realized you were my friend, so I didn't bite you."

American golfers in the booze aisle at Tesco:

"That one sounds classy, look, it's European. What's it called? Stella Artoys?"

Girl: "My academic mom is coming to town."
Boy: "Who was she again?"
Girl: "You know, the one that used to study medicine but then joined the circus and is now touring with them."

Outside library:

"I didn't notice until I put the cake in the oven. Then the phone rang...from the oven."

Maths Microlab:
"I mean it's not stalking or anything, she writes to him in German so I just copy and paste their conversations from facebook into the German translator. I just like to keep an eye on what they're talking about..."

Inebriated academic family member:
"...And Vishnu's really, really, really good at table tennis."

David Russell Apartments:

"May Dip? Why can't they change it to October dip?! I want to go running into the sea whilst my body is still banging from the summer."

" Girl 1: "Do you want to know what happened last night in halls? It's disgusting."
Girl 2: "What?"
Girl 1: "So, someone took a dump in an oven and then cooked it."
Girl 2: "Unbelievable."
(Silence)
Girl 3: "Do you reckon it was someone in halls, or someone from John Burnet?

Tourists/ Locals/Kids

In St Andrews Botanic Gardens, with Junior garden group. 8 Year old gets his hair caught in a tree:
"CURSE YOU, you confounding branches!"

> **Little girl (around 8 years old), Market Street, Raisin Sunday 1pm (sighing):** "Its because they are all drunk."

Tourist on Market Street at Midnight:

"I hear there is a great club called the Lizard, and its even open all week, we could go every night!"

American Woman: "Well, we've sure seen a lot of Scotland. It's not as angry as I thought."
Male Companion: "I know, I've only been punched once so far."

Elderly couple about to set off down the Travelator:
Old Man (offering his arm): "Hold tight!"

Second hand book shop on Market Street:
Small child reading the book titles: 'Woman in White.' What's that about?
Father: "To my shame, I have never read it."
Small child: "Maybe it's about a woman who wears white."
Father: "Well don't spoil it for me."

Woman hurrying out of M&Co to her four/five-year old child: "I told you three times, if you swear at people you won't get any sweets!"

Child: "You cheeky bitch!"

On Greyfriars:
American golfer 1: "Did you see that?"
American golfer 2: "No what?"
American golfer 1: "That kids just standing there smoking a joint, I've not seen that since the 60's!"

Group of tourists in front of B&B on North Street at 10:30pm, deciding where to go: "Well the clubs don't get busy until around 2..."

Guy on The Gaudie after his torch blew out:

"Now I just look like a s**t wizard."

Guy talking to his friend on North Street: "Jesus could never have come from Glasgow... they wouldn't have been able to find a virgin and 3 wise men."

American girl: "Shinty? Is that a religion?"

May Dip, guy 1 to guy 2 in wetsuit:
"YOU ARE MY SON, AND YOU WILL DO IT NAKED."

Mother to child on Market Street:

"Only good girls get toys...not absolute f*ing nightmares."**

By the old course hotel:
"it's a nice hotel, but I mean it's Scottish nice, not nice nice."

From the University of St. Andrews May Dip article on Wikipedia:

"Many of the town's residents hope for some type of simultaneous tidal wave event."

Mum and little girl on South Street outside Miller's Tale
Little girl (to black labrador): Bye-bye doggie!!
...
Little girl (to mother): Mummy! He didn't say 'bye-bye' back!

American tourists outside the quad:
"I'm really disappointed... its nothing like in that Wills and Kate movie."

Middle aged local guy in Tesco angrily saying to some girl:

"What do you mean you've never had Irn Bru ???"

> **Young English girl outside Tesco standing in the rain with her daddy:**
> **"Daddy... do they have a summer here?"**

St Regs Ball:
American Girl: "You have a really sexy English accent."
Guy ignoring this chat up line: "I'M FROM F***ING GLASGOW YA PRICK."

Mother and young boy standing in Boots:
Mother "oooo false eyelashes for only £2.99"
Son *pleading*: "Can I have some?"
Mother *laughing*: "If when you're older you still really want them, then I'll get them for you".

An old man in the tesco checkout buying a crate of stella and a copy of FHM with the biggest grin on his face to the cashier:
"My wife's away for 2 days"

> **Saturday lunchtime, an elderly lady walking past a group of guys dressed in various combinations of oktoberfest/st patrick's outfits:**
> **"They're going to have a shock when they get out into the real world."**

Little boy feeding the Kinnessburn ducks: "Freedom! Freedom for all the ducks!"

Just walking past the PH on North Street, a French guy explaining it to his two friends:

"On the 1st of March, they do this thing called the May Dip..."

Drunk guy walking past Tesco this morning at 5 to two Tesco employees having a cigarette break outside: "Good morning." Both replying at the same time "Good night!"

Two girls outside Costa who clearly hadn't seen each other since the summer holidays start shrieking and hugging each other. Old man walking by: "Oh for Christ sake -- calm the f* down."**

> **American tourists on West Sands**
>
> "I think I can see Ireland!"

A guy and a girl both from Northern Ireland, near the bus station, having a conversation about potatoes:
Girl: "have you ever grown potatoes??"
Guy: "yeah I have, have you??"
Girl: "YES... I love potatoes, they are glorious!!!"

Group of new students lost on South Street, one approaches a local for assistance:
American girl: "Excuse me sir, can you help us find..?"
The local (who was a woman): "Why did you think I was a sir?"

Barman in Edinburgh: "I went to visit St. Andrews, it was great- the only bad part is that I brought the wife."

A girl and a boy are walking hand in hand in church square, discussing the moon:
Boy: "You know, the moon never orbits. The side we see is the side we'll always see."
Girl: "Oh my god! So what's on the other side??"
Boy (enigmatically): "'... more moon...'"

In Tesco:
Mother: "Shut up!"
5-year-old son: "No! You shut up, you old maid!"

Elderly woman on a bike at the Argyle Street roundabout/free for all immediately after getting cut up by a boy racer in a Mitsubushi Evo:

"Oh, you f***er!"

Two Scottish 40ish year old men, talking seriously about wildlife documentaries at the ATMs outside Tesco...
Man 1: "Mm, they're so interesting. Do you know what a reindeer has that no other animal has?"
Man 2 (intrigued): "What?"
Man 1: "A baby reindeer. Now tell me that isn't funny."
Man 2: "F***ing prick." *walks away*

Little boy and his mum in line at Tesco:
Mum: "Did you get an advent calendar?"
Boy: "Yes, and I'm going to get 3 more."
Mum: "3 more?"
Boy: (solemnly) "Yes, 4 sweets a day."

Madras girl in Tesco.
"Do you think it would be pretentious to buy sushi for lunch? I mean, I don't even like sushi. I just want to be seen eating it."

In restaurant, choosing from the menu:
Golfer 1: "Ooh, this dish sounds very good, I think I'll try that one."
Golfer 2: "Oh dear no! It's not nearly expensive enough ... Go on, have this expensive one, it'll be good for you!"
Golfer 1: "Ahh, very good point."

Woman in the Post Office queue morning after raisin on her phone:

"So then I woke up, and someone had s**t on the car, and I burst into tears, and then the fire brigade showed up – can I send these First Class? – and it was quite a night, I tell you that much."

Happy looking man holding a large golf umbrella on South Street:
Man: "Are you enjoying your St. Andrews holiday?"
Wet wife:...*angry glare* "...What do you think?"

Outside Tesco: "It's bloody HERB! With an 'H'!!"

> **Walking down lade braes beside Reg's Annex:**
> "You can tell that graffiti was by locals and not the students."
> "Why?"
> "Because they spelt it wrong."

Guy in the Vic: "I think it's just a midgie bite."
Other guy: "But I haven't seen any midgets around here!"

Conversation with an overseas student in the Lizard..
Student 1: "Where are you from?"
Student 2: "Germany"
Student 1: "Whereabouts in the UK is Germany?"

Group of Americans near the Whey Pat:

"OMG this is the worst fake town ever... I mean look at these cobbles. They are soooo fake."

Some drunk Glaswegian guy at raisin:
"MA NAME'S PAUL... I'M AT UNI."

> **Irish guy: "In Ireland we put a potato on top of the tree instead of an angel."**
> **Girl: "What really????"**

Guy 1: "I heard you shouldn't drink the tap water here because it has high levels of estrogen."
Guy 2: "Eh, I've lived here for years and I haven't grown boobs yet, so I think it's fine."

Lecturer to student in Tesco: "You can tell the students are back in town as all the half price wine is gone."

Walking away from Tesco, Madras girl picks up a receipt from the ground: "Ugh, you can tell they're students; everything they've bought is organic."

Two middle aged female tourists on Market Street, "The Marks and Spencers must be around here somewhere!"

Group of Asian tourists outside the castle where you can see the scaffolding:

"They're rebuilding the castle!"

Guy unlocking his bike on South Street, casually as you like:

"St Andrews is kinda like a massive city stuffed into a shoe."

Middle aged woman outside Morrisons:

"I totally did'y recognise you with your clothes on!"

Small child walking past puddle of water coming from Tesco fridges: "SOMEBODY had an accident..."

"I think in Scotland c*** means, like, person."

Taxi driver to people who had ran across the street in front of him
"Next time, I will run you down!"

Americans looking out from East Sands:
"How beautiful! Look, there's Norway!"

American guy proudly sharing his knowledge of Scottish wildlife:
"And I think I also saw a yak!"
Girl, trying to be patient:
"I think you mean a highland cow..."

Woman to her 5 year old on Bell Street:
"BECAUSE NO ONE EATS ICE CREAM FOR BREAKFAST!"

American girl in Kinburn Park:
"You'd think St. Andrews would be too cold for palm trees."
-while passing the yucca plant

American woman trying to pay for the shuttle service from Glasgow airport to the City Centre:
Woman: "Do you accept dollars?"
Driver: "No"
Woman : "Do you accept euros?"
Driver : "No."
Lady : "Can I pay you with a combination of euros and dollars?"

A girl outside Lloyds:
"I saw some guy get pushed into the sea buy a girl in red, there were like 10 guys in suits watching."

Three madras kids coming out of 'Ultimate Party' around lunchtime:
"I...I don't think I ever want to go in there again..."

Middle aged American guys on Greyfriars:

"Yeah so where's this Wizard? How do we get to the Wizard?"

> **In Superdrug:** "When my bf cheated on me, he made up for it by buying me a KFC! It was cold and the chips were soggy, but it's the thought that counts. I hadn't had a KFC in months!"

"B-I-E-utiful!" – a builder on some scaffolding

Young woman: "No, no, no. If you had a cat you'd just kick it about the flat all day."
Elderly woman: "Oh honestly, that was ONE time."

Boy on Muttoes Lane: "Cake, Dad! Cake?"
Father: "No son, it's called KEG."

Elderly woman on Church Street: "Are there any charity shops in St Andrews?"

1 Golf Place at lunchtime:

Tourist 1: "What country is Scotland in again? Europe?"
Tourist 2: "I think it's its own country"
Tourist 1: "Nah, you're thinking of Yorkshire"

> **Girl pointing to the caravan park above east sands asks:**
> **"Is that Dundee?"**

On the train back up from London after reading week, coming into Leuchars. 2 old ladies:
Lady 1: "I wonder why there are so many young people getting of here..."
Lady 2: "I don't know [reads station sign]"Leuchars for St Andrews" say, isn't there a University of St Andrews? That sounds familiar."
Lady 1: "No, don't be silly I'd have heard of it. I think there's an RAF base here. That's where they'll all be headed."
Lady 2: "Aaah okay."

"There are only so many excuses for which being Irish is valid."

Made in the USA
Charleston, SC
25 October 2012